Sex & Babies

FIRST FACTS

For GVB, with love — JA

For LMN, with love — MN

To Tony, with love — DO

For my exceptional family - MTP

Published by
M A G I N A T I O N   P R E S S
An Educational Publishing Foundation Book
American Psychological Association
750 First Street, NE
Washington, DC 20002

For more information about our books, including a complete catalog,
please write to us, call 1-800-374-2721,
or visit our website at www.maginationpress.com.

Editor: Darcie Conner Johnston
Art Director: Susan K. White
The text type is Bookman
Printed by Phoenix Color, Rockaway, New Jersey

Library of Congress Cataloging-in-Publication Data

Annunziata, Jane.
Sex and babies : first facts / written by Jane Annunziata and Marc Nemiroff ;
illustrated by Denise Ortakales and Maureen Tracy Patrolia.
p.   cm.
Summary: Text and illustrations explain the male and female body,
conception, pregnancy, and birth. Includes a note to caregivers and glossary.
ISBN 1-55798-809-9 (hc : alk. paper) — ISBN 1-55798-808-0 (pbk : alk. paper)
1. Human reproduction—Juvenile literature. 2. Sex instruction for children.
[1. Reproduction. 2. Sex instruction for children.]
I. Nemiroff, Marc A. II. Ortakales, Denise, ill. III. Patrolia, Maureen Tracy, ill.
IV. Title.

QP251.5.A56 2002
612.6—dc21   2002005616

Manufactured in the United States of America
10 9 8 7 6 5 4 3 2 1

FIRST FACTS

written by
Jane Annunziata, Psy.D.
Marc Nemiroff, Ph.D.

sculptured paper illustrations by
Denise Ortakales

drawings by
Maureen Tracy Patrolia

MAGINATION PRESS • WASHINGTON, DC

What is sex?

Sex is a word that can have different meanings. There are two main definitions:

1 *Sex can mean a person's **gender**, which is either male (gender symbol = ♂) or female (gender symbol = ♀).* In other words, sex can refer to whether someone is

a boy

OR

a girl

2 *Sex can also mean a special kind of touching that adults do together when they love each other and want to be close.*

When people talk about "sex" or "having sex," they are usually talking about this special kind of touching.

Let's begin with gender.

The most important thing to remember about males and females—boys and girls and men and women—is that they are like each other in many ways. In fact, they are more alike than they are different.

All people have most of the same body parts, inside and outside. And all people have the same kinds of thoughts and feelings. They can share the same hopes and dreams. They want to do the same kinds of things when they get older.

But there are some ways in which males and females are not alike. When you look at this picture of the male and female bodies, you can see where they are different.

These differences between males and females make two things possible:

1 having sex

2 having a baby

Let's take a closer look at the male and female bodies.

THE CHEST

Both males and females have two **breasts** with nipples on their chests.

When grown-up women become mothers, their breasts are able to make milk to feed their newborn babies.

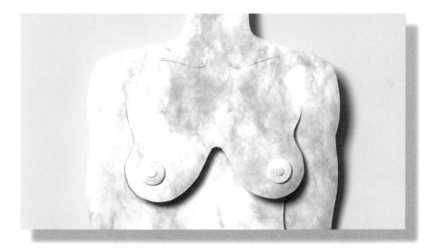

Females: *The breasts become larger and rounder as girls grow up. This usually starts to happen when a girl is somewhere between 10 and 13 years old. It can also happen earlier or later.*

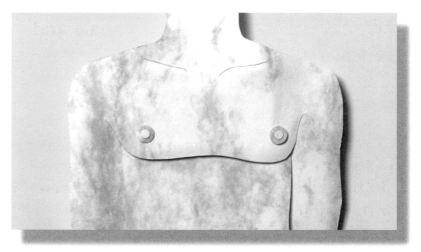

Males: *The chest area usually becomes broader and more muscular, but the breasts remain flat as boys grow up.*

THE GENITALS

Each sex has its own set of **genitals**.
These are the organs or body parts that
make a boy or man a MALE, and a girl
or woman a FEMALE.

Most of the male genitals are easy to see
on the outside of a male body.

Penis: *a long, tube-like organ that is
between the legs. The penis hangs
over the scrotum.*

Scrotum: *a pouch beneath the penis that
contains a pair of testicles.*

Testicles: *two round organs inside the scrotum
that make **sperm**. Sperm float in a
thick fluid called **semen**. Sperm help
make a baby.*

Urethra: *a long, thin tube inside the penis.
Its opening is at the tip of the penis.
Both urine (which comes from the
bladder) and semen pass out of the
penis through the urethra—but never
at the same time.*

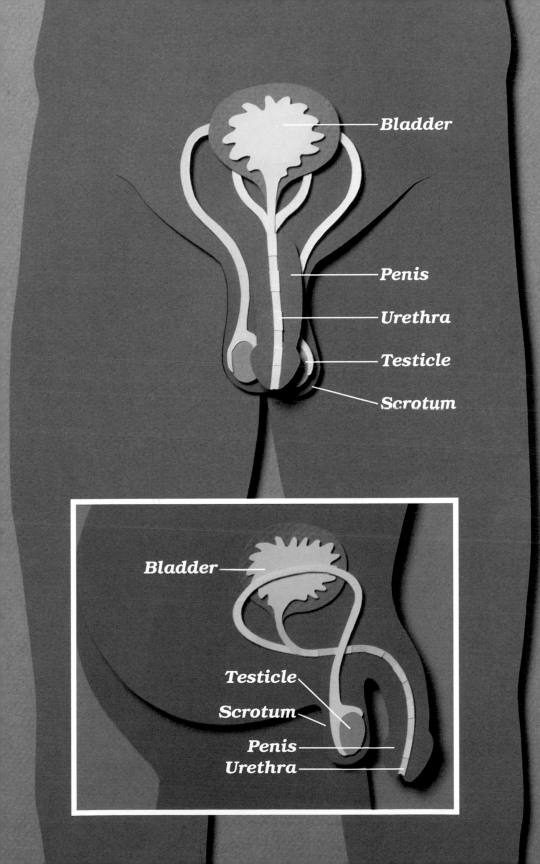

Bladder

Penis

Urethra

Testicle

Scrotum

Bladder

Testicle

Scrotum

Penis

Urethra

Most of the female sex organs are on the inside of the body, where we can't see them.

Uterus: *a sac where a baby grows until it is ready to be born.*

Ovaries: *a pair of oval-shaped organs that contain **eggs**. An egg helps make a baby.*

Fallopian Tubes: *a pair of thin tubes, each leading from an ovary to the uterus.*

Vagina: *a long tube that goes from the uterus to the outside of the body, between a female's legs.*

Vulva: *the part of the female genitals that we can see. The vulva includes the folds and small mound of skin around the opening of the vagina.*

Urethra: *a thin tube that carries urine from the bladder out of the body. The urethra is not one of the sex organs in females, but it is located very close to them.*

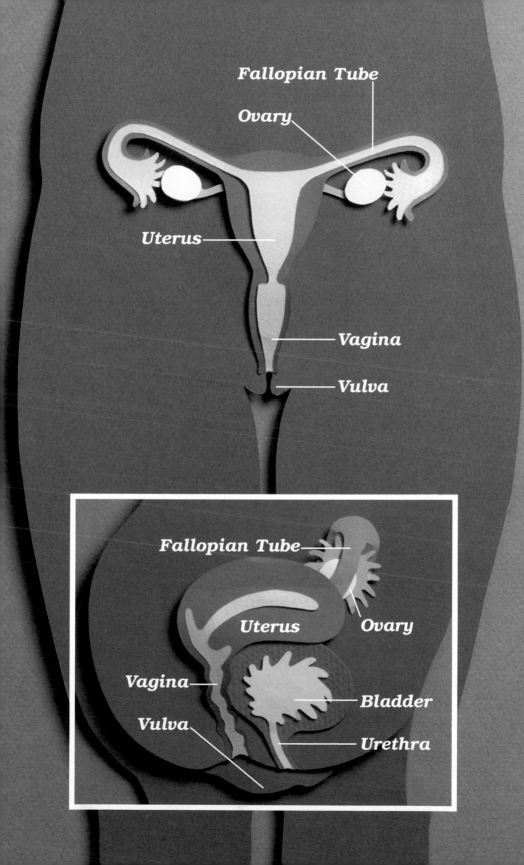

Fallopian Tube

Ovary

Uterus

Vagina

Vulva

Fallopian Tube

Uterus

Ovary

Vagina

Bladder

Vulva

Urethra

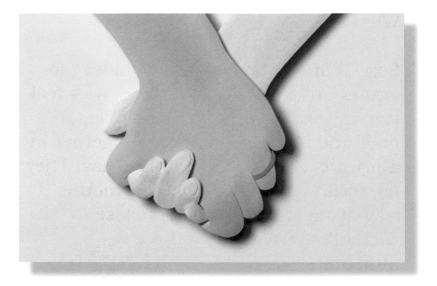

Now let's talk about having sex.

Teachers and doctors usually say **sexual intercourse** when they talk about having sex, and we will too in this book. Many people simply call it "making love," because it is something that adults do when they love each other.

Sexual intercourse is something that two adults do when they are in a special relationship such as marriage. They are a couple. They care very much about each other, and sometimes want to show their love in a physical way.

14

What exactly is sexual intercourse?

Sexual intercourse is a natural way for adults to say "I love you" when they feel love in their bodies. It begins when a man and a woman are alone together in a private place. They hug and kiss. They are feeling intimate, which is another way of saying they feel very close to each other. These intimate feelings cause their bodies to change.

The man's penis, which is usually soft, becomes stiff. This is called an **erection**. The woman's vagina gets softer. During sexual intercourse, the man puts his erect penis inside the woman's vagina, as they continue to hug and kiss each other. Soon the man or the woman or both may have a pleasing sensation called an **orgasm**. When a man has an orgasm, a small amount of the fluid called semen comes out of his penis. This is called **ejaculation**. After orgasm, sexual intercourse is completed, but the man and woman continue to enjoy feeling close.

What are YOUR feelings?

Young people are often very curious about sex. They usually hear about it from other people and from movies, magazines, books, and television. They may have a lot of questions, because some of the things they hear may seem confusing. Asking an adult you trust, such as your parents or the person who gave you this book, can be helpful when you have questions about sex.

Sometimes children feel embarrassed when they learn about sexual intercourse, and they think that adults must feel embarrassed too. It is natural to feel this way, because our bodies are private. So it may be difficult to imagine that when adults love and care about each other, they don't feel embarrassed and they enjoy being together in this way.

Children may also wonder if sexual
intercourse feels uncomfortable or hurts.
They may even worry about it. But it is
not uncomfortable. In fact, it feels quite
nice, and afterward the couple feels
relaxed and happy.

So, men and women have sexual
intercourse because it allows them to
show their love and because it feels good.
And sometimes a man and a
woman have an extra reason:
they want to have a baby.

SEXUAL REPRODUCTION

The scientific term for having a baby is **sexual reproduction**.

Sometimes when a man and a woman have sexual intercourse, all of the basic building blocks needed to create a baby come together. This doesn't happen every time they have sex. But when it does happen, we call it **conception**.

The basic building blocks for creating a baby are an egg from the woman and a sperm from the man.

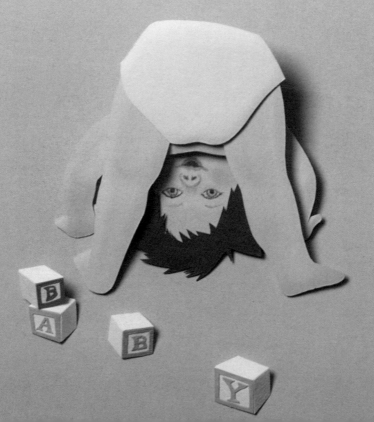

When a man and a woman are having
sexual intercourse, the semen that comes
out of the man's penis contains millions
(yes, millions!) of sperm. They are so tiny
that you can see them only with a
microscope. Through a microscope, they
look like tadpoles with long tails that
help them swim in the semen.

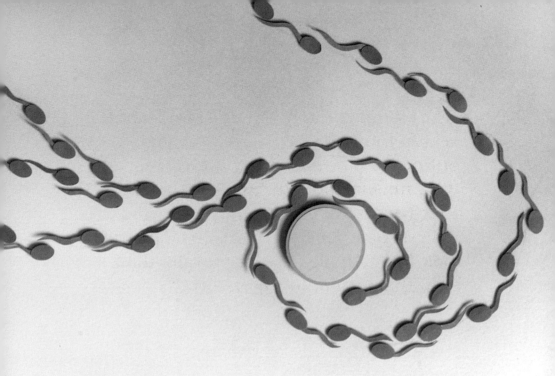

When sperm are in the woman's vagina,
they begin to swim and search for an egg.
A woman's egg is much bigger than a sperm,
but you still need a microscope to see it.

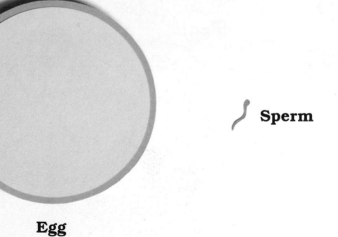

Sperm

Egg

Sperm swim up the vagina and into the uterus, which is located at the top of the vagina. From there, they swim into the two fallopian tubes that are attached to each side of the uterus. Then they swim through the fallopian tubes, toward the ovaries at the end. The ovaries contain the woman's eggs.

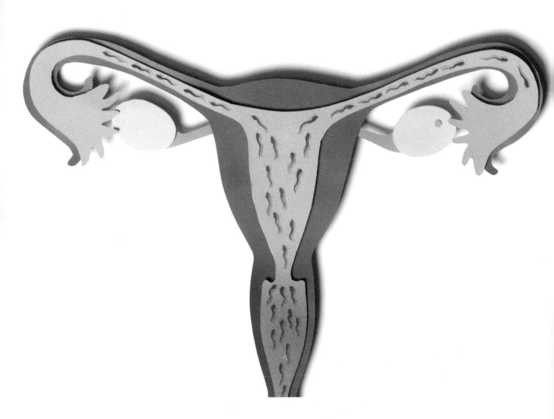

CONCEPTION

About once a month, one of a woman's ovaries usually sends an egg into the fallopian tube. The egg travels down the fallopian tube toward the uterus. If any sperm are swimming in the fallopian tube at the same time, the egg and one sperm can meet and join together. When this happens, we say that the egg has been *fertilized*. Conception has occurred.

Sperm gather around an egg

One sperm wiggles inside the egg

The egg is fertilized

The woman is now **pregnant**. As you probably know, this means a baby is starting to grow inside of her body. She is the baby's mother. The man whose sperm fertilized the egg is the baby's father.

After conception, the fertilized egg moves down the fallopian tube and into the uterus, where there is plenty of room to grow. The uterus will be the home for the growing baby until it is ready to be born.

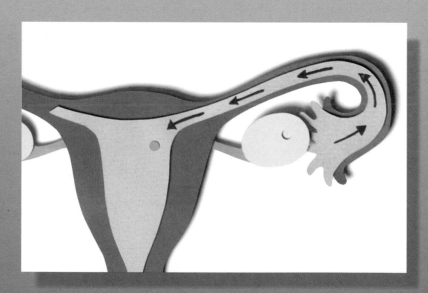

It takes about nine months for the fertilized egg to grow into a fully formed baby.

At first it looks like a tiny ball. It takes about three months for all of a baby's body parts, such as arms, legs, ears, and eyes, to form out of the ball. Then the baby spends the next six months growing bigger and stronger.

The baby needs food in order to grow. The mother's body feeds her baby through the **placenta**. The placenta is an organ that grows with the baby and is attached to the inside of the mother's uterus. Food from the mother's body goes to the placenta, and then is carried to the baby through a long tube called the **umbilical cord**. The umbilical cord attaches to the baby in the middle of its belly, in the spot that will become the baby's belly button, or navel, after he or she is born.

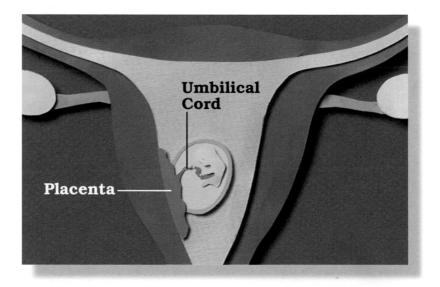

Umbilical Cord

Placenta———

A Look at the Growing Baby

AT ABOUT 6 WEEKS

Six weeks after conception, the baby is about the size of an adult's thumbnail. Even though it is so small, quite a lot has been happening. The eyes, ears, and heart are forming. You can already see the start of the elbows, arms, and feet.

AT ABOUT 3 MONTHS

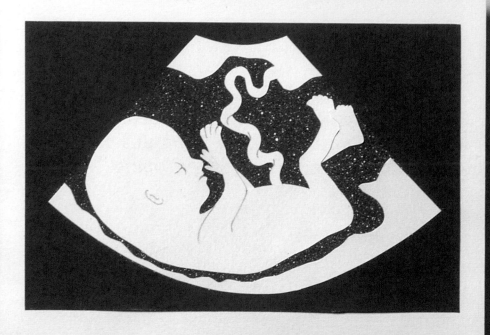

This is the actual size of the baby.

The baby is three times as large as it was six weeks ago. It is now more than $2\frac{1}{2}$ inches long curled up, and it weighs at least half an ounce. That's about the weight of four grapes.

Almost all of the baby's body parts are present by this time. Of course, they continue to develop and grow.

Doctors can see and take pictures of the baby using a sonogram machine, and they can hear its heartbeat with another machine called a doppler. The heartbeat is about twice as fast as an adult's and sounds much like a horse galloping.

Also:

The brain is developing into the "control center" of the body.

The skeleton is forming.

The baby is moving its mouth, hands, and feet.

The fingers and toes are visible.

The genitals are starting to take shape.

AT ABOUT 4 MONTHS

At this age the baby is about 5 inches when curled up and weighs more than 5 ounces. That's about as heavy as a small banana.

Very fine, silky hair is growing on the baby's body, especially on the head. The fingernails are now developed, and the baby can move its arms and legs. Many mothers start to feel these movements now. This is very exciting! Other people begin to notice that the mother is pregnant, because her belly is growing larger.

This is the actual size of the baby

Now the baby is more than 9 inches long when curled up, just about the size of the baby in this picture. It weighs almost 2 pounds, or about as much as a quart of milk.

Placenta

This picture shows the baby in its *amniotic sac*. *Amniotic fluid* fills the sac and surrounds the baby, so that the baby floats. The amniotic fluid and sac serve as a "shock absorber" so that the baby doesn't get bumped. Amniotic fluid also helps keep the baby at the right temperature.

He or she is starting to look like a newborn baby.

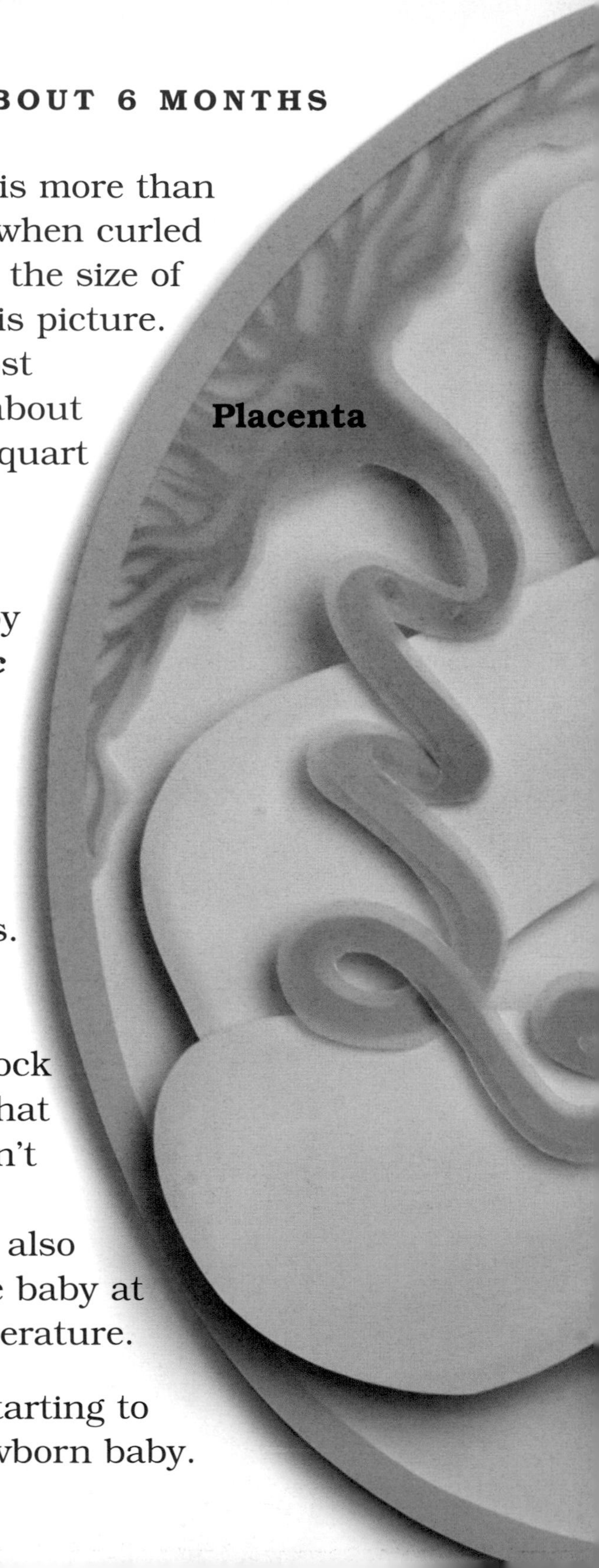

Amniotic Fluid

——— **Umbilical Cord**

This is the actual size of the baby

AT 7 MONTHS

The baby is now about 11 inches long curled up, and as much as 18 inches long from head to toe. It weighs about $3\frac{1}{2}$ pounds and continues to look more and more like a newborn baby. It is developing eyelashes and eyebrows and isn't as skinny-looking as it was a month ago.

This picture shows how the placenta connects to the baby with the umbilical cord, how long the umbilical cord is, and how large the placenta is in comparison to the baby.

AT 9 MONTHS

The baby at nine months is ready to be born. It is about 20 inches long from head to toe. Most babies weigh between 6½ and 8 pounds when they are born. At this time, the baby is fully developed, inside and out. Most babies are now in the ready-to-be-born position, with their heads down, waiting to leave the uterus.

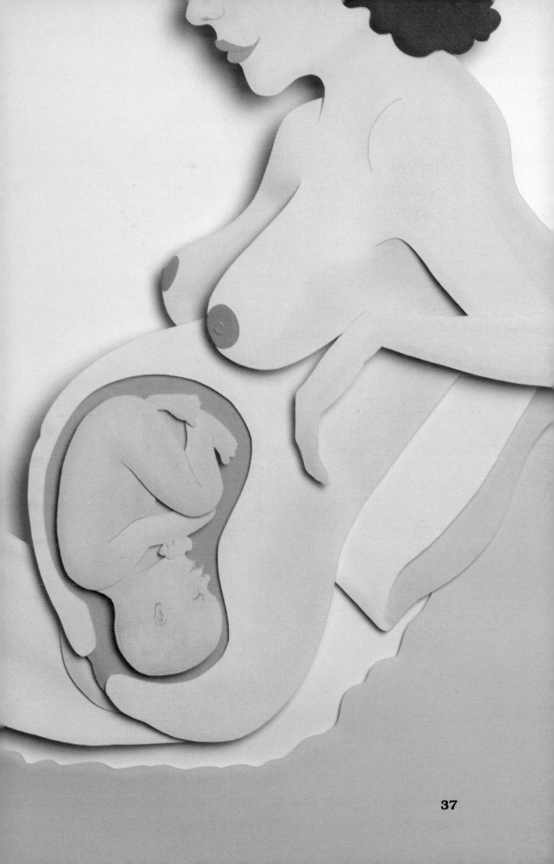

BIRTH

The mother's body usually knows when the baby is ready to be born. Most babies are born in a hospital, where doctors and nurses are there to help. Usually the father also helps the mother by staying with her, comforting her, and making sure she has everything she needs.

The process of giving birth usually takes several hours. This process is called **labor** because it is a lot of work. Labor starts when the muscles in the mother's uterus begin to squeeze. The muscle-squeezing starts slowly and gently, and gets stronger and stronger, until the baby is finally pushed out of the uterus, down the vagina, and out of the mother's body.

The birth isn't over quite yet.

The umbilical cord is still attached to the baby. The doctor, or another person such as the father, clips the cord close to the baby's body. The baby can't feel this. It's like getting your hair or your fingernails cut.

The umbilical cord isn't needed any more since the baby can now drink milk from the mother's breasts or a baby bottle.

The birth of a baby is a thrilling moment. The mother and father get to look at their baby for the first time. They hear its voice as it cries and starts to breathe. They touch its fingers and toes. And they can see the sex of their baby, who will grow into...

a girl

or a boy

...like you.

Glossary

Amniotic fluid: the fluid that surrounds a developing baby in the uterus while its mother is pregnant. The amniotic fluid cushions the baby from bumps and jolts, and helps keep the baby at the right temperature. *(pages 32-33)*

Amniotic sac: a thin but tough layer of tissue called a sac or membrane that holds the amniotic fluid and the developing baby in the uterus. *(pages 32-33)*

Breasts: a pair of organs on the chest. Women's breasts are larger and rounder than men's breasts, and women's breasts produce milk for feeding newborn babies. *(pages 8-9, 40)*

Conception: the beginning of pregnancy, when a sperm and an egg join together. *(pages 19-23)*

Eggs: stored in a woman's ovaries, an egg is needed, along with a sperm from a man, to create a baby. Although a woman's ovaries contain thousands of eggs, the ovaries normally release only one egg per month. This is why women usually have one baby at a time. (Twins are born when the ovaries have released two eggs at the same time and sperm are present.) *(pages 12-13, 19-24)*

Ejaculation: the passing of a small amount of semen out of the penis during a man's orgasm. A man is said to *ejaculate* during orgasm. *(page 16)*

Erection: a term that describes a man's penis when it becomes stiff. An erection is necessary for sexual intercourse to occur. *(page 16)*

Fallopian tube: one of two long, thin tubes that connect a woman's ovaries to her uterus. An egg travels from an ovary to the uterus through a fallopian tube. *(pages 12-13, 22-24)*

Fertilization: the action of a sperm joining with an egg. The sperm is said to *fertilize* the egg. *(page 23)*

Gender: the sex of a person, either male (symbolized by the sign ♂) or female (symbolized by the sign ♀). *(page 4)*

Genitals: the organs or body parts that are different in males and females. The genitals are the organs used in sexual intercourse and sexual reproduction. *(pages 7-8, 10-11, 12-13)*

Labor: the process of giving birth. When a woman is giving birth to a baby, she is said to be *in labor.* *(page 39)*

Orgasm: a pleasing sexual sensation that both men and women can experience. *(page 16)*

Ovaries: a pair of female genital organs that contain a woman's eggs. The term *ovary* comes from the Latin word *ova,* which is another name for a woman's eggs. *(pages 12-13, 22-23)*

Penis: The long, tube-like organ on the outside of the body that is part of the male genitals. *(pages 10-11, 16)*

Placenta: an organ that supplies food and other needs to the developing baby in the uterus. The placenta grows with the baby and comes out of the uterus after the baby is born. *(pages 26, 34-35)*

Pregnancy: the term used to describe the condition of a woman who has a baby developing in her uterus. A woman is usually *pregnant* for about nine months. *(page 24)*

Scrotum: a sac of skin that hangs under the penis and contains the testicles. *(pages 10-11)*

Semen: a thick fluid that comes out of a man's penis during ejaculation. A few drops of semen may contain many millions of sperm. *(pages 10, 16, 20)*

Sexual intercourse: a special form of touching, involving the genitals, that men and women share when they want to be close to each other. *(pages 14-16)*

Sexual reproduction: the process of *reproducing,* or creating a new person (a baby), that is made possible by joining an egg from a woman with a sperm from a man. *(pages 19-26)*

Sperm: produced by a man's testicles, a sperm is needed, along with an egg from a woman, to create a baby. A man's testicles normally produce millions of sperm every day. *(pages 10-11, 19-24)*

Testicles: the pair of male genital organs, located under the penis in the scrotum, that produce sperm. *(pages 10-11)*

Umbilical cord: a tube that delivers food from the placenta to the growing baby in the uterus. *(pages 26, 34-35)*

Urethra: a long, thin tube in both males and females that urine passes through when traveling out of the body. In males, the urethra runs through the penis and is part of the genitals, because semen and sperm travel through it to exit the body. *(pages 10-11, 12-13)*

Uterus: a stretchy sac inside a woman's body where a baby develops and grows until it is ready to be born. *(pages 12-13, 22-24)*

Vagina: part of the female genitals, a tube that goes from the uterus to the outside of the body. *(pages 12-13, 16, 21-22, 39)*

Vulva: the part of the female genitals that we can see on the outside of the body. The vulva includes the folds and small mound of skin around the opening of the vagina. *(pages 12-13)*

Note to Parents

Sex is about as fundamental to life as food and shelter, work and love. From an early age, we are naturally curious about our bodies, and we can feel physical pleasure. We notice that male and female bodies are different, that people kiss and hug each other, that babies are born. If not for sex, of course, we wouldn't exist at all. But more than a matter of mere biology or survival, sex can be a very enriching part of adult life.

Because sex is so integral to our being, it is important that children receive their first information about it in a positive, age-appropriate way. The way the topic of sex is handled sets the tone for how children will feel about it in the future, and how comfortable they will feel about sharing their questions and concerns as they get older. When parents provide the right information at the right time and in the right way, they help their children develop healthy attitudes toward their bodies and their relationships with others for the rest of their lives.

SEX IS HARD TO TALK ABOUT

Many parents feel unsure when it comes to talking with children about sexuality. Sexuality and sexual relating are private, personal, and emotionally sensitive areas for adults. Thus, by definition, the topic is hard to share with *anyone*, and parents may be especially uncomfortable about discussing it with a child. Talking about sex makes a private parental activity feel public in the family, and this can be awkward. It makes parents feel that kids now know what's going on behind closed doors!

Parents may also find it difficult to talk about sex because they're afraid they won't know how to answer the questions they imagine their children will ask. In fact, questions will come to the child's mind, and ideally children should feel comfortable voicing them. They are the child's attempt to fine-tune the basic knowledge that he or she has just learned. Parents may be relieved to know that the questions are generally not as difficult as they fear, and that answering them may not be as difficult as they imagine.

And finally, some parents may worry that discussing sex with their children will lead to experimental sex play. Keep in mind that almost all young children engage in sex play or exploration of some kind—either by themselves or with peers—because they are naturally curious. They are seeking information. Thus, it is all the more important that children receive accurate and appropriate education about sex from their parents.

CHILDREN FEEL AWKWARD TOO

It may be helpful for parents to know that children have many parallel discomforts when talking about sex. They have been brought up to understand—correctly—that our bodies are private, so they too feel awkward and embarrassed.

Children are often quite put-off and surprised when they first learn the details of sexual relations. They may think it sounds strange, or even aggressive or disgusting. The idea that sex can be pleasant and enjoyable (and voluntary!) is hard to grasp. It is important for parents to communicate a positive view to children, however, in order for children to develop their own positive attitudes about sexuality and later positive feelings about sexual relating.

Pregnancy and childbirth may also be a difficult topic to discuss, especially if a parent or child fears childbearing as unpleasant and painful. It is helpful for all children to learn that pregnancy can be a happy and exciting experience, that the birth process can be comfortably managed, and that holding a newborn baby is among life's most joyful events.

THE BASICS: WHAT TO SAY AND HOW TO SAY IT

Here are some basic points to keep in mind as you talk with your child about sex and babies.

Use the right words. Always use the correct words for body parts, sexual activities, and aspects of reproduction. When you do this, you communicate a matter-of-factness that helps kids hear the information with less embarrassment. When parents are matter-of-fact, kids are more likely to believe that this is indeed like any other topic their parents have taught them, and not something weird or scary.

That said, parents are often uncomfortable saying the words *vagina, ejaculation,* and so on, and they may be tempted to use more vague, less accurate words instead. But this only tends to confuse kids when they later learn the correct words for these body parts and sexual activities. They may feel embarrassed and babyish that they have been using a euphemism, and also wonder why they weren't given accurate information to begin with. The result is a general sense that something is different or bad about this topic. So even if you have to practice saying the words aloud (or

reading this book out loud to yourself), do whatever it takes to reach a point of adequate comfort.

Start early. When should parents start talking about sex? Parents can lay the groundwork from the time their children are hardly more than babies by teaching them the right words for body parts during potty training and bathing. In this way, children are already comfortable with words such as *penis* and *vulva.* Also, if potty training, bathing, and other body matters have been handled in a positive, matter-of-fact way all along, parents will have a relatively easy time segueing into conversations about sex and babies.

As for information about sexual relations, a good rule of thumb is to respond to your child's questions as they come up, rather than imposing a schedule of education. Children hear things, see things, and even feel things in their own bodies. They see images in the media. Their older siblings or other children may be telling them what *they* know. You or another family member or a neighbor might be having a new baby. Usually, children will want to ask questions when they are confused or ready to know more. Respond to questions in simple and age-appropriate terms, confining your responses to the question at hand but communicating an openness to further inquiry.

For example, a child who asks, "Why do only married women have babies?" might be perfectly satisfied with, "Usually that's the case, but sometimes other women have babies too." On the other hand, the child may then ask, "But *how* does a woman have a baby?" and a longer conversation can follow, with the parent staying sensitive to the child's levels of interest, understanding, and comfort.

Thus, parents are not talking about sex just once. Rather, they need to be sensitive to when children want new information, when they need a repetition of information, when they need clarification, and when it is time for discussion at a more mature level. In this way, learning about sex and babies is an ongoing process. The important thing is to create an environment in which talking about sex feels as comfortable as possible—where children feel they can always ask questions and receive honest, helpful answers.

Use books as a tool. Books such as *Sex & Babies: First Facts* are available for children at many age levels, and are an ideal tool for talking with children and imparting reliable information. They are a springboard for conversation, they give parents the words to use and a structure and format for conversation, and they help parents know what aspects of sex a child of a particular age might be ready to learn about. Finally, books with pictures give both parent and child something to look at and focus on, which may help both feel more comfortable.

For young children, especially those whose parents are introducing another baby into the family, several good offerings present sex and reproduction in soft, simplified terms, usually in the form of stories about mommy, daddy, and baby. *Sex & Babies* is suitable for children who are approximately 8 to 12 years old: children who probably know a little bit but need to have many holes filled in and perhaps some misinformation and distortion corrected. Unlike books designed for younger children, *Sex & Babies* is fact-based. The tone is

intentionally somewhat dry, because children at this age are less embarrassed when the information is less personalized. The illustrations, too, were designed with the reader's comfort in mind; they are clear and informative, but not graphic.

Sex & Babies provides the basic information needed for sex and reproduction to make complete, logical sense. Many topics are not covered, including puberty, menstruation, masturbation, sexually transmitted diseases, homosexuality, birth control, and the mechanics of sexual pleasure. Children can learn about these more complex issues as they mature, and there are a number of good books and other resources available to help families when the time comes.

In particular, information about sexually transmitted diseases should not be included with early information about sexual relationships and reproduction. While educating older children and teenagers about diseases is very important, it is best to keep the topic separate. This way, children do not merge in their minds the beauty and intimacy of sexual relating with worries and fears about illness or disease.

Monitor your child's receptivity. Be aware of your child's level of interest. A child's level of receptivity will change with different aspects of the material. For example, it is much easier for children to hear about gender differences and the development of a baby than to hear about the specifics of intimate sexual relations.

You may want to read the book in sections, dividing the information to make it more manageable and digestible for kids. Too much information often creates anxiety in children, and they can become easily overwhelmed. This is especially possible with such a complex and personal subject as sexuality.

Monitor your child for indications of anxiety or information overload. Signs might include squirminess, nervous laughter, increased distractibility, boredom (including yawning), asking unrelated questions, or changing the subject. If any of these occur, or even if you're not sure, discontinue the reading. Your child may indicate readiness for more by directly asking questions or by looking at the book (which you have left out or within easy reach). Or you may overhear him or her talking about sex with other children.

Encourage dialogue. As you read and discuss the book together, encourage your child's questions about sexual relating and reproduction. You might simply ask your children if they have any questions about what they are hearing. You might also give your child permission to ask questions by saying something like, "Sex is something that kids often have lots of questions about. You can always ask us any questions about anything, either now or later."

Questions about sexual relating and reproduction should (hopefully) increase as the child matures. As children get older, their questions become more specific and require more detailed answers. At younger ages, however, it is important to keep answers honest, basic, and simple. For example, if your 8-year-old says, "You have three kids, so does that mean you had sex three times?" you might say, "No, grownups have sex whenever they want to be close to each other in a physical way, not just when they want to make a baby."

Parents often don't know how to respond to questions from younger children about such things as oral sex or homosexuality. Don't raise topics that younger children haven't brought up themselves, but do be prepared for the fact that these topics may come up.

If you are asked, "Why are those two men holding hands?" it is best to say something simple, such as "Usually a couple is a man and a woman, but sometimes it is two men or two women. They also want to be close to each other." If you are asked, "What is oral sex?" you might answer an 8-year-old with: "That is a special type of grown-up sex. As you get older, it will be easier for me to explain it to you." You could give a 10-year-old a little more information: "It is a kind of adult sexual relations. It is a special type of kissing that involves the genitals." If a child persists, it's best to say something like, "This is what you need to know now; the rest we can explain when you are a little older." Please note, however, that some 10-year-olds already know a few details of oral sex and may be upset and confused by it. They will need their misinformation clarified, the correct details provided, and the adult nature of this activity stressed.

Finally, it's perfectly fine to say that you're not sure of the best way to answer a question and that you'll think about it and get back to the child with an answer. Take the time you need to think through your response, get accurate information, check with a professional if in doubt, or resolve your discomfort with the topic. Just be sure to return to the child's question without him or her having to remind you.

JANE ANNUNZIATA, PSY.D.
MARC NEMIROFF, PH.D.

About the Authors

JANE ANNUNZIATA, PSY.D., is a clinical psychologist with a private practice specializing in children and families in McLean, Virginia. She serves on the clinical faculty of George Washington University's Doctor of Psychology program. As a writer, she has contributed parent guidance sections to many children's books on such topics as shyness, parental depression, and a new baby in the family.

MARC NEMIROFF, PH.D., serves on the core faculty of the Washington School of Psychiatry's Infant and Young Children Mental Health Training Program and the clinical faculty of George Washington University's Doctor of Psychology program. He is also an Affiliate Member of the Baltimore-District of Columbia Society for Psycho-analysis, and he maintains a private practice for the treatment of children in Potomac, Maryland.

Dr. Annunziata and Dr. Nemiroff are the authors of *A Child's First Book About Play Therapy, Help Is on the Way: A Child's Book About ADD,* and *Why Am I an Only Child? Sex & Babies: First Facts* is their fourth book together.

About the Illustrators

DENISE ORTAKALES has loved cutting and crafting with paper since childhood. She holds a degree in illustration from the Art Institute of Boston, and teaches art at McIntosh College. Her award-winning paper sculpture illustrations have enlivened the pages of children's magazines such as *Spider, Ladybug,* and *Cobblestone,* as well as many grown-up publications, including *Consumer Reports* and the *Utne Reader.* This is her third children's book. She lives in New Hampshire with her husband and two sons.

MAUREEN TRACY PATROLIA is an accomplished portraitist and landscape artist with a degree in illustration from the University of Massachusetts in Dartmouth. Also a preschool teacher, she says that her work is often inspired by her young students, as well as her many nieces and nephews. She lives in Plymouth, Massachusetts, with her husband and two dogs. This is her second book.